Dean Chambers and Craig Brown

DISCLAIMER: The material provided in this book should be used for informational purposes only and should not be relied upon for financial advice. Also, note that such material is not updated regularly, and therefore, some of the information may not be current. Please be sure to consult your own financial advisor when making decisions regarding your financial management.

ISBN: 978-1-7772242-0-2

Table of Contents

Table of Contents (cont...)

Author's Note

I grew up in Jane and Finch where the future for the youths is bleak and the life expectancy of Black males is short. I wasn't very studious—who I am kidding? I hated school. But they always told us that education was the way out. I needed education if I wanted to make it out of the "hood." I needed education so I didn't become a "waste yute" (a youthful person who is a waste of time and space; a young person who doesn't make proper use of their time and energy). I didn't want to be a statistic and I had goals that I wanted to accomplish. I went to college, where I studied accounting and finance to make my mom proud. I graduated and got a great job as an auditor with a major company. I was comfortable and doing well for someone my age.

Fast forward 5 years later, and one day, I got a call that I will never forget. My boss had called me into his office to let me know that our department had been downsized and that I would no longer have a job. I had never been let go from a job before. As he spoke, I could no longer hear what he was saying because all I could think about was what I was going to do. It was a scene out of the Peanuts cartoon where the teacher just says "womp womp womp womp womp." In addition to being let go, I was about to get married and I had a daughter to support. My mom had taught me a thing or two so I had some savings, but I didn't know what my next move would be. Still, I was down but not out.

Anyone that knows me knows that I am disciplined with my money—and that saved me. Another thing that worked in my favour is that I had a second stream of income. BUT, I was not going to rely on that. I swore to myself that I would figure a way out and that I was never going to work for the man again! I began to brainstorm about all of the things I was good at and other ways I could generate income. I went back to an old venture and brought it to life and opened my own car dealership. Easy? Hell No! Worth it? Of course! Now entrepreneurship isn't for everyone, but it is what worked for me.

Whether you work for yourself or work for a company, you too, can attain financial literacy and freedom. I am not a financial advisor, but I know a thing or two about money, they don't call me cheapskate for nothing.

I've never had a handout, and I didn't have a trust fund or get a head start in this life. I started where you might be today. I am living proof that your beginning doesn't have to be your end. Come with me on this journey and don't be a waste yute!

- Dean Chambers

Introduction

"Financial Literacy" is a commonly used term that I, for one, am not very fond of, and this is why. The first time that I heard it I had no clue what it meant; I had zero connection to the term. When you hear that phrase, what comes to mind? Math? Language? Reading?
Money? If you are not familiar with the term, or have heard it but have no clue what it means, then you're in luck. This book will help you learn the basics. Although "financial literacy" might sound complicated, it really just describes one's knowledge of money; how money works, and how to use it to your advantage. Now you may ask, "what do you mean by 'how to use it?'" It seems straight forward, right? Get money, spend money. Those of us who have been around the block a few times know how to make money (getting a job) and the ways that we have to spend it (shopping/paying bills). The main goal behind financial literacy is to help you maintain your money. Who wants to work their whole life just to pay bills? To live check-to-check? How about staying in debt and then passing it onto one's child(ren)? No one does! That's why we have to become financially literate. For these reasons, most of us understand that one makes money through working a job, which involves trading your time for money, and spends it on bills, recreation, and other costs of living. The one thing we're often not so good at, is responsibly maintaining the money we earn. The goal of this book is to help you understand some basic concepts of money that they don't teach you in school. I think that people of all ages should know the basic concepts when it comes to money. There is no age limit. I wish I knew then what I know now—cliché but true. Being financially literate is one of the keys to success in our modern world. Success is defined as the achievement of a desired goal. You, too, can attain success if you follow the advice contained herein.

So, what is money? Money is nothing more than a marker that you can trade for other things like food, shelter, clothing, etc.— the list goes on and on. But money takes a long time to save, especially if you do not earn a lot. When you want to make a large purchase like a house or a car, money can only go so far. To make such a purchase, you will need another tool—a loan. A loan is an agreement where someone (a borrower) receives money in advance and repays the other person (the lender) by an agreed-upon date in the future. As an incentive for lenders to offer loans, they are usually compensated in the form of interest.

Despite the borrowers' best-laid plans, however, lending out money comes at a risk—the risk that lenders will not get it back. Whereas you might decide to lend your friend money because you trust them to repay you, the banks don't know us that way. So, how can lenders judge who is likely to repay and who is not? That is where credit scores come in. They tell lenders how "creditworthy," or how reliable a borrower has proven to be.

A person with good credit and only a little cash is in a much better position than someone who has a lot of money and bad credit. Why? Well, it's because most people cannot afford to pay for some of life's biggest purchases—like houses and cars, for instance—in cash. Have you heard the saying, "don't burn your bridges"? Well, this is one bridge that you definitely don't want to burn, because it can affect you for a very long time. Plus, you will have an easier time moving ahead and getting what you want financially, if people are willing to lend you larger sums of money at lower interest rates.

Ultimately, banks and businesses exist to make money. Let's say you want to buy a house. You will go to a bank and apply for a loan to purchase this house. So that you can live in your house now—instead of when you have all of the money saved up—you make a contract with the bank promising to repay what you borrowed within a certain time frame. Now let's say you were late on two payments and missed one. You just broke the agreement that you made with the bank, which now tells them that you cannot be trusted to pay the loan back. A few months later, you decide to get a car loan, but because you broke your first agreement with the bank, they are less likely to say yes. If they give you a loan anyway, it will probably be at a higher interest rate, meaning that the bank collects more money, the worse you are at paying on time.

So, how does one obtain credit? Every time that you enter into an agreement as a borrower, the lender will report your repayment activity to the three major credit bureaus: Equifax, Transunion, and Experian. Credit bureaus are the companies that track your debt and your repayment. As you enter into more agreements—another credit card or line of credit, a car loan or a mortgage, department store credit, or student loan debt—you begin to build your creditworthiness. If you consistently make payments on time, you start to develop a positive relationship with these companies, which is similar to a good report card. On the other hand, late or missing payments are like negative report cards: there's going to be some trouble somewhere down the line.

Throughout the book, I talk about the four major areas of financial literacy: savings, credit, financial planning, and investing, to help you better yourself with the financial life lessons I have learned. Common sense is not common where money is concerned, and so, this book aims to clarify misconceptions and build a solid foundation for financial success. Inside, you'll find:

Chapter 1 – Savings: Are You Stupid, Are You Dumb? Savings is a Must!!!!

In this chapter you will learn the basics of saving and why it is so very important. Life is unpredictable, and in order to be prepared for unexpected adversity, you've got to have savings. Having savings provides you with a sense of security, and let's be honest, it is kind of nice to see a stack of cash or lump sum in your bank account. But don't get it twisted; as good as it makes you feel to see large amounts of money stacking up, saving is not something you do to "flex" (show off) with new purchases like fresh new kicks, high fashion clothing, or jewelry. Once you reach your first savings goal, you shouldn't want to spend it. You should want to see it double or even triple! There is an art to saving, and if you read this chapter carefully, it will help you get into a position where you'll always have something set aside for a rainy day!

Scenario: The car breaks down

Your vehicle gets you from point A to point B in a time-efficient manner. Without it, you'll find yourself unable to complete your Amazon orders as a part-time gig. Now you're faced with a dilemma if you don't have savings: I need money to fix the car, but I need a car to earn money. As a rule of thumb, saving 5-10% of your pay over a period of time will allow you to have enough money saved if an unexpected incident were to occur.

Chapter 2 – Investing Don't Cheese Me... Make Your Money Work Harder with Wise Investments!

In this chapter, I plan to try and open your eyes to the numerous opportunities available to make your money work hard with minimal effort on your part!!! After reading this chapter, you will be equipped with the knowledge to allocate your money across various investments carefully selected by you.

Scenario: Your coveted Air Jordan 1's Red & Black (1984)

Let's say you purchased these highly coveted exclusive releases for $300. And now a month later, you sell them for $1,500 on StockX.com. You just made $1,200 from your initial purchase (buy low and sell high).

Chapter 3 – Credit: Issa Vibe

In this chapter, you will learn the importance of achieving a great credit score. In addition to learning the different types of credit available to you, you'll see why cash is not king... credit is!!

Scenario: Making moves

Were you hoping to get your own crib? What about a nice whip? With bad credit (or no credit) you cannot attain or make life-changing investments such as a real estate purchase or a loan to build your business. When you have good credit, it can allow you to make upfront purchases for your new business while holding onto previously earned money. The key to credit is using other people's money to build your wealth!

Chapter 4 – Financial Planning “Differently”: Financial Planning is Well Worth It, Eh?

Most people say you either “Fail to Plan or Plan to Fail.” Which side of the coin are you on? Having an additional stream of income can help you reach your financial goals faster. In addition to a regular job, a second, or even third source of income can bring in cash flow without trading more of your time for more money. The time you take to prepare your finances will make all the difference when checking off your weekly financial boxes! This chapter will take you through a few simple strategies to help you achieve your financial goals.

Scenario: Gotta have it

You finally come up with an idea and decide that a vending machine is what you would like to purchase; you even have the perfect location to house this machine. So, you put together your financial plan (budget) to help you attain your goal and you discover that it will take you approximately 3 months to get together enough money to purchase your investment. Clearly document what is needed to achieve your purchase goal. Look at your expenses and your net pay for the next 6 paychecks (bi-weekly pay) to see what you can limit or eliminate from your variable expenses (wants) and put away the funds needed to purchase the unit.

Take these lessons to heart and get your money right!

Chapter 1

Savings: Are You Stupid, Are You Dumb? Savings is a must!!!!

Savings play an important role in the state of our finances. Since we can't predict the future, saving money can help us to become financially secure and provide a safety net in case of an emergency. "What type of emergency?" you might be wondering. You should save up for things like a new roof for your house, out-of-pocket medical expenses, or a sudden loss of income. When something unexpected happens, if you do have a credit card, that's the first place you'll go. By saving money in advance, you can avoid going into debt to pay for necessities when life doesn't go as planned.

To help you in unexpected circumstances, you should create an **emergency fund**. A good emergency fund will hold three to six months of living expenses—enough for everything from rent, utilities, and car loans, to gas, groceries, and toiletries. So, if you generally live on $3,000 a month, you'll want to save anywhere from $9,000 to $18,000 for your fund.

If possible, open a high-interest savings account that will earn you money as you save (see more below). Avoid accounts with monthly fees, as that will decrease your savings.

Now maybe you're thinking, "Crap! How can I possibly save that much money in cash?" Before you start googling the organs that humans can live without, however, consider using the below strategies.

Ways to Save

1. Pay yourself first.

   - A lot of times, you'll hear people say that you should pay all of your bills first and put the remainder into savings. I want you to put that advice aside. To ramp up your savings, pay yourself first. That means that when you receive your paycheck, multiply your net deposit by 0.10 (10%) and that's the amount you should put aside weekly/biweekly. For example, if you make $500 every two weeks, you should be saving $50 each check. Treating your savings like a commitment instead of an afterthought will help you save faster and more consistently.

2. Apps and programs that round up your spending.

- There are various apps like Mylo that specialize in helping you save without really thinking about it. On every purchase, these apps can round up to the nearest $1 or $5 and transfer the remainder to a savings account. By adding up this "spare change," the more you buy, the more you save. Consider asking your bank about which program they would recommend.

3. Find ways to cut costs and save money.

- Coupons, clearance, and cashback programs like Flip, Checkout51, or redflagdeals.com can help you save a lot of money on things like groceries, gas, and other everyday purchases. PC optimum is a great program to earn points for gas and groceries.
- Try to limit optional expenses like beauty and entertainment. If you can't eliminate an expense completely, consider cutting down your frequency. It might seem impossible to go without your manicure or your trip to the barber, but going half as often could seriously improve your savings. Buy off-brand products where possible.

4. Kick a habit.

- Do you spend money each week on alcohol, cigarettes, marijuana, or other recreational substances? Do you have to have your Starbucks every morning? Can you cut one of them out? Maybe smoke less or share cigarettes or skip a night out? Make coffee at home? Habits can get expensive quickly, and because we rely on them, we often fail to realize how much money they're consuming. If you can kick a habit, save the money you would've otherwise spent on it.

5. Save windfall money.

- When you get "windfall," money—also known as "found" money—or money you weren't expecting, always save it. That tax return? Save it. A birthday check from mom and dad? Save it. Saving unexpected funds allows you to reach your goals more quickly without disturbing your regular spending.

6. Open a high-interest savings account.

- Savings are necessary, but they're also static. The money just sits there, and the bank lends it out to other people in the form of loans. If this isn't the right time to invest your money, try to put it into a high-interest or high-yield savings account. Such accounts may offer anything from 0.5% to 3% interest on your savings, allowing you to make money by holding onto what you already have.

7. Wait on impulse buys.

- You know how a lot of our parents bought that exercise bike from a television commercial, only for it to become a clothes hamper that no one ever uses? Or maybe how you bought that new pair of sneakers you saw on Instagram, even though you have three other pairs in your closet that you don't wear? We buy these things and never use them because they are impulse buys. Unlike necessary purchases, impulse buys seem really important at the time but later don't make as much sense.

- To reduce your number of impulse buys, adopt the 5-day rule. If you want something outside of your budget, wait 5 days from when you first have the idea. If you still want it after 5 days, it probably isn't an impulse buy. But if the luster fades and you find yourself moving onto a new shiny object, it stands to reason that maybe you can live without it.

8. Create a savings plan.

    - If you struggle with saving money, building out a savings plan may help you stick to your goals. In the Appendix (C) to this book, you'll find a 52-week savings goal sheet that takes one large goal and breaks it down into smaller amounts. Smaller amounts make it much easier to save and allow you to track your progress as each week passes.

9. Get a side hustle.

    - Finding an additional source of income is another way to increase the amount of money that you have to save. If you can, monetize your skills and interests, turn them into a business, and watch those extra bucks roll in. See Appendix B for a list of businesses that you can start with little to no money.

But savings aren't only for emergencies; there are other goals that you might want to save towards, too, like your own house, a new car, college tuition, and retirement.

In general, even when you aren't saving for something big, the best practice is to save 5 to 10% of your annual income.

Chapter 2

Investing: Don't Cheese Me... Make Your Money Work Harder with Wise Investments!

So, you've reached your goal of three to six months savings for your emergency cash fund. What's next?

It's important to remember that wealth is rarely built by simply saving money. Wealth can only be achieved when your money starts making money for you. That is what investing is: letting your money do the hard work for you. While you can only work x number of hours per day, your money, if properly invested, can work for you 24 hours a day doing whatever you tell it to. It's almost like your dollars and cents become little soldiers. The more you have deployed, the more progress they'll make. Treat investing like your job! When you work for someone else, you can be sure that you'll put in a hell of an effort to keep that paycheck coming in. You have to do the same with investments! Put time and effort into learning because your mind is your biggest asset and knowledge is power!

When you open a regular savings account, you might earn interest—or a return for placing your money in the bank—at a rate of somewhere between 0.01% and 0.1%. This means that if you deposit $1000, in a year, you'll probably earn between $0.10 and $1.00 in interest. That's not very much extra money. When you invest, however, you earn interest at a quicker rate. Investing creates compound interest, "the interest you earn on both your original deposit and on the interest you continue to accumulate" (Armstrong). According to Lance Cothern from Money Under 30, "The benefit of higher compounding returns is you won't have to invest as much each month as you would need to save each month to reach your goal." Sounds good, right?

So how much more quickly can we expect to earn more money if we invest? To figure that out, we refer to a handy trick called the

"Rule of 72," which tells us how long it will take to double our investments. You divide 72 by your interest rate and the answer is the number of years it will take to earn double. So if you earn 6% on your investments, it will take 12 years to double the initial amount. If you earn only 3%, it will take you 24 years. Those who understand the rule make it. Those who don't, pay it.

Different types of investments will have different rates of return and will come with different types of risk. Here, we'll discuss stocks, bonds, mutual funds, and real estate.

Stocks

Stocks represent a way of buying into a company's success by investing in a piece of their business. While private companies—enterprise companies—do not sell stock to the general public, publicly traded companies do. To buy these pieces—called **shares**—and to know how much they're worth, investors participate in the stock market.

When a company goes public, they turn ownership of the company into a pie and divide it into a certain number of pieces, or shares. The pieces set aside for sale to the public are sold on the **stock market** at a certain value—determined by a lot of factors that we'll return to—and so anyone with enough money can buy however many shares in the company they desire.

What stocks are best for:

Personally, I see stocks as best for long-term investments. There are many ways to make fast money on stocks. **Daytrading** is the process through which people buy and sell stocks every day to try and sell for higher than they just bought. You may see higher returns this way, but you're also taking a greater risk because stock prices go up and down on a daily basis. This means that the more frequently you trade, the harder it is to plan for profits and losses. If you hold on to stocks for a long enough time, depending on the type of company, the value can go up exponentially.

NOTE—if the price of the stock is below what you paid for it, your stocks are worth less in value, BUT you are not at a loss until you sell them. The same holds true for your stocks if the value is higher than what you paid.

Here's an example:

> Let's think about a company like Amazon. They started out as an online bookseller, and their first public stocks were $18/share (Shen). Now, Amazon is one of the biggest companies in the world. Right now, Amazon stocks go for over $2,000/share. So, let's do the math. If you bought 100 shares of Amazon in 1997, you spent $1,800. If you held on to all of those shares until now–never sold any of them—the same shares would be worth over $200,000 today. That means that in a little more than 25 years, you would have made roughly 110 or more times your initial investment. Can you see how buying and selling the right stocks at the right time can earn you big bucks?
>
> In the same breath, though, not all stocks increase in value. Let's say Amazon was a flop instead. Those shares that were originally worth $18 each are now worth $1 each. That means that although you invested $1,800, you're only left with $100 if you try to sell them now. You can try to hold onto them in hopes that the price goes back up, but if it doesn't, your investment is gone. A $1,700 loss is a big deal because in this case, it would have been better to put your money in a savings account.

Who Stocks Are Best For:

The greater the risk, the greater the reward... or the greater the loss, depending on how things turn out. Stocks are best for people who can determine their own **risk tolerance**—how much they can afford to lose. But instead of losing it all to figure out how high that tolerance is, savvy investors try to figure out which companies are riskier to invest in than others BEFORE they buy. A stockbroker is someone who buys and sells stocks for their clients. Professionals like daytraders have to be exceptionally knowledgeable about the sale of stocks to make a profit. But you don't necessarily need a

stockbroker to invest wisely. The most important thing is to do your research. Make sure that you know the relevant information on the company you plan to invest in, including their 5-year plan, their financial statements, their dividends (if any), and any legal matters currently in effect—anything that could lower your stock price. Remember that since stocks are often based on **speculation**—people's public opinion of what the company will be worth—unexpected bad press could lead to a drop in their stock value.

It's All About the Dividends, Baby

The value of an individual stock goes up and down until you're ready to sell it. Selling it for more than you bought it for creates profit, sometimes called capital gains. But some stocks also make their investors money in the meantime. Stocks that pay **dividends**—or a share of the company's yearly profits—reward shareholders quarterly for holding onto their stocks.

Dividends will be calculated per share. So, for example, if one share were to yield $50/quarter in dividends, someone with 10 shares would get $500/quarter. Even more than buying and selling, dividends are a serious way to increase your investment.

For example,

> Warren Buffet is one of the greatest investors of our time, both because he has invested in high-dividend stocks (such as Apple, Bank of America, Wells Fargo, Coca-Cola, Kraft Heinz, American Express, US Bancorp, JP Morgan Chase, Delta Airlines, and General Motors) and because he has held onto them for a very long time. In 2020, it is estimated that Buffet will earn roughly $4.7 billion on dividends alone. This means that not including the value of the stocks themselves, he's making $4.7 billion this year on the profit from his various investments.

So, what should you do with your dividends? The best advice that I can give is to reinvest your dividends back into the business. This compounds your investment quickly.

What's the difference between principal, ROI, and dividends?

The **principal** is the amount of the initial investment. For our Amazon investor, the principal was $1,800.

Dividends are quarterly profits distributed to shareholders. So, with their 100 shares of Amazon, let's say the same investor gets $50/quarter ($200/year) for each share (100 shares); the investor would bring home $20,000/year in dividends.[1]

In this case, a principal investment of $1,800 yields the investor $20,000/year. Now THAT is letting your money do the hard work for you.

The **ROI** is the amount gained on an investment relative to the initial investment.

ROI = Net Profit/Total Investment * 100

Net profit = $20,000-$1,800 = $18,200
Total Investment = $1,800

18,200/1,800 * 100 = 1011%

In this example, the ROI for the initial investment is 1011%. Can you imagine having even one investment like that? How about a dozen?

Tips for New Investors:

- Do your research, including a company's 5-year plan, their financial statements, their dividends (if any), and any legal matters currently in effect—anything that could lower your stock price.

[1] DISCLAIMER: This example uses exaggerated figures to simplify and clarify examples of dividends. While there are some companies that pay very high dividends, the majority will offer a significantly lower quarterly return than is suggested by the figures here

- Look for stocks that pay dividends (and at how long they've been paying dividends for)
- If you do not know what stocks to buy, start with companies whose products or services you are familiar with.
- Buy low, sell high
    - This means that with thorough research, you should be able to pick stocks that are currently low-priced but have a lot of potential for high returns.
    - Hold on to them until the stock price rises and sell when the value is high.
- Avoid penny stocks
    - The value of penny stocks can change significantly from an increase or decrease of just pennies and may either change very quickly in value or not at all.

Bonds

Bonds are a type of investment where you're lending a company or government money and they pay you an interest rate in return—remember, interest is the fee lenders charge to others for borrowing money. The interest rate is usually fixed, which means that it won't fluctuate over the term of the loan. Further, bonds mature, meaning that they MUST be repaid to you by a certain date.

In addition to government bonds, you can also buy fine art bonds or collectible bonds—anything that has long-term value.

What do they use the money for? The organizations that offer bonds use the invested money for public projects and operations. Because they often need more money than individual banks can loan, bonds allow individuals to contribute as lenders.

CDs (Certificates of Deposit)

CDs are like bonds in that they represent an amount

loaned by an individual to an organization with the understanding that the organization can use it however they want, for a set period of time. But where bonds are offered by companies and governments, CDs are offered by banks and credit unions, so they may be a more profitable alternative to a savings account as long as you don't need to touch the principal until the term is over. Bonds are longer-term investments while CDs are shorter term, but both require you to leave the principal alone or pay high fees.

Who Bonds & CDs are best for:

If you have a lump sum that you won't need to touch for a while, bonds and CDs are both safe ways of investing that represent diversification. **Diversification** is the practice of investing in different types of things so that if one area does poorly, there are other investments to fall back on. Those looking to diversify their investment portfolios (set of investments a person makes) might consider bonds and CDs for long-term stability. You won't make as much as you would with stocks, but you also take less risk, and still generally make more money than you would by putting the same amount into a savings account.

Mutual Funds

Mutual funds, like bonds and CDs, put a bunch of individuals' investments together to work with a larger amount. But where bonds and CDs are organized by companies, governments, and banks, and distributed by application, mutual funds are managed by money managers who allocate the funds across different types of asset classes (stocks, bonds, and other assets) to make a profit for the investors.

When you invest in stock, you become a shareholder and get a vote on how the company is run. But when you buy into a mutual fund, you get a share of the profits from what the managers decide to buy (portfolio) instead of direct profit from the price of a single company or their dividends. A share of a mutual fund contains many stocks and other investments, while stocks are direct shares of a given organization.

Then why would I invest in mutual funds instead of stocks?

Well, stock value is determined by the worth and performance of a company. So, if you buy 100 shares from one company and that is your only investment, your risk is higher because you stand to lose everything if they fail. In the same breath, it is often too expensive for small-time investors to buy full shares in enough different types of companies to be safe if one fails. In this case, a mutual fund would allow you—an individual investor—to diversify your portfolio without buying multiple costly shares in multiple companies.

So how do I make a profit with mutual funds?

Because they often contain stocks, mutual funds can still pay dividends. Of course, the return is smaller than it would be if you owned full shares in a company, but you will be likely to receive dividends from more companies this way. Where stockholders only get dividends if that company profits, mutual fund investors will generally see more frequent and consistent returns. The fund can also make capital gains (selling assets for more than their purchase price), which would be distributed to the fund holders. Lastly, you can sell your shares (partial though they may be) on the stock market.

Real Estate

Real estate is often considered the safest type of investment because land almost always appreciates (goes up in value). That being said, real estate is also a costly investment.

The best strategy is to buy when you can, with a selling price in mind, and sell the property when it reaches your desired value. But costs of maintenance, renovation, and the state of the housing market may ultimately prevent you from cashing out the value of your property when you want to.

Another profitable way of investing in real estate is buying a property and renting it at a rate high enough to pay the mortgage and make a profit. This way, you receive spendable money (cash flow) each month while essentially maintaining the property for free.

Example: Let's say you buy a house for $200,000 on a 30-year mortgage loan with a down payment of $20,000. Now, let's say your monthly mortgage is $1,100/mo, but you can rent this new house for $2,200/month. Each month, you're making $1,100 profit. Within 18 months, your renter has paid back your initial down payment of $20,000, and everything else you make in the future (above the cost of the mortgage) is pure profit. You can also earn money on your home through capital gains. When you're ready to sell, a profit will help you with your next investment.

Equity

When you buy a house, you have **equity**—a term that means you have an asset against which you can borrow. So, let's say you need to send your kid to college. If you need to, you can borrow against the equity in your home, taking a loan relative to its worth. If you fail to pay it back, your home serves as **collateral**—something of value that may be confiscated in case payment stops. While borrowing against one's home isn't always the smartest idea, equity means that you have something valuable to bargain with.

In a similar vein, you have equity from your life insurance policy. When you pay into a life insurance policy, it will grow in value as the years go by. Insurance companies will allow you to borrow against your policy, giving you something of value to offer as collateral.

Risks and Rewards of Different Investment Types:

Stocks

Upside: Stocks offer individuals voting power and many provide access to company profits (dividends), allowing a higher return on investment

Downside: Stock prices fluctuate oftentimes based on speculation (people's feeling about what might happen), leading to high risk

Bottom-Line: Stocks are versatile and may offer short-term gains and/or long-term security but are susceptible to the stock market and represent high-risk investment

Bonds

Upside: Bonds offer a structured investment opportunity with guaranteed repayment of the principal (not so in stocks) and yield higher interest than savings accounts

Downside: Fluctuating interest rates may lower the value of the bond below the initial purchase price

Bottom-Line: Bonds are safe fixed investments with low risk and comparatively low yield

Mutual Funds

Upside: Mutual funds allow individuals to diversify their investment portfolios at a lower cost, allowing more sources of security

Downside: Profits are smaller, and funds are unprotected by the FDIC

Bottom-Line: Mutual funds are lower risk than stocks but higher risk than bonds, offering more opportunities for diverse returns but risking everything if poorly managed

Real Estate

Upside: Real estate appreciates (gets more valuable) over time and may serve as a physical asset that also provides equity

Downside: Requires a large initial investment and fluctuations in the housing market threaten the owner's ability to sell at a profit

Bottom-Line: Real estate is the safest type of investment and can have short-term payoff but can grind to a halt as a source of revenue if the housing market crashes

Chapter 3

Credit: Issa Vibe

So, finally, we come to the most commonly misunderstood aspect of personal finance: credit. What is credit? Well, credit is essentially an agreement where someone (the borrower) receives something of value and agrees to repay the other party (the lender) at or by an agreed-upon date in the future. As an incentive to lenders, borrowers are generally charged interest—or a fee for borrowing—as a form of compensation.

Why do we need credit? As we discussed in previous chapters, it is very difficult to save enough money upfront to buy some of life's biggest expenses. How long would it take you to save $15,000 cash for a car or $200,000 for a house? What would you drive and where would you live while you were saving? If we could only obtain the things we can buy with cash, most of us would go half a lifetime without owning anything of significant value. Credit allows us to enjoy the things that we can't afford in full right now while paying them off over time.

Here are a few other things that you'll need credit to do:

- Buying a new cell phone or signing up for a new cell plan
- Renting an apartment
- Financing a funeral
- Getting car insurance
- Getting a credit card
- Financing furniture (like Rent-A-Center)
- Financing jewelry
- Getting a business loan
- Applying for a job

While cash has many benefits, cash is not king—credit is! In the same breath, however, credit becomes **debt**, which is the obligation created when you accept borrowed money.

Now that we understand what credit is, it's important to review how and under what circumstances credit is granted. The most important determining factor for credit is a person's credit score. A **credit score** is a measure of how likely one is to pay a lender and/or creditor on time and have the resources to do it consistently. Your credit score is like a financial report card that lists a record of how much you've borrowed, how much you've paid back, and how many times you've sought new lines of credit. Credit scores range from 300 (poor) to 800+ (excellent). **Creditworthiness** is determined by looking at this report card. Unfortunately, every time that you request credit from someone new, your credit score drops a little—but we will return to this later.

When a lender loans out money, they want to minimize the risk that they won't be paid back. That is why credit scores are used. They are generally a good indicator of a person's ability to manage debt, which is why a person with a bad credit score but a lot of cash is worse off than a person with a great credit score and less cash. The better your score, the more that companies feel comfortable loaning money to you on the good faith that you'll pay it back. At the same time, credit score determines interest rates as well. To further offset risk, lenders charge higher interest rates (a larger fee) to people with lower credit scores. Let's look at two situations:

Situation #1: A borrower with an excellent credit score wants to request $10,000 credit. The lender is relatively certain that they will be paid back in full and on time, so they grant the money at an interest rate of 10%. That means that when you borrow $10,000, you'll end up paying $11,000 back to compensate for the use of the money when you didn't have it.

Situation #2: A borrower with a poor credit score wants to request the same $10,000 in credit. In this case, however, the lender is uncertain about how frequently the borrower will be able to pay or if they'll be able to pay off the full amount at all. So, if the lender decides to give this person the $10,000 loan, they will likely offer a higher interest rate—let's say 25%. This means that the borrower will have to pay back $12,5000 over the lifetime of the loan.

From these scenarios, you can see that the better your credit score is, the cheaper it is to borrow money. The more trustworthy that lenders find you, the less they'll charge you in interest, and vice versa. High-interest rates are one of the main reasons that people stay in debt because you can often end up paying back twice as much as you borrowed. If you can only make minimum payments, it will be impossible to pay off a large sum. So, you can see the benefits of having a high credit score. The higher your score, the more money you can borrow at a cheaper rate. Your credit score will affect things like personal loans and credit cards, but also things like the ability to get a mortgage or car loan.

Types of Credit

This brings us to the types of credit. There are three different types of credit that you can apply for. There are **revolving credit** accounts, which are lines of credit (up to a certain amount) that you can use over and over again. A credit card is a revolving account because once you pay your balance, you can spend the same amount of money on credit next month. Next, there are **installment accounts**, which have a set due date for payoff. When you go to buy a house, you'll have a mortgage payment each month structured for you to pay back the entire borrowed sum within 20-30 years. The same holds true with car payments. If you receive something upfront but only own it after it is paid off, it is an installment account. Lastly, there is **open credit**. The least common of the three, open credit is like revolving credit in that you can use it over and over once the balance has been paid off. It is different from the others insofar as you can spend an unlimited amount of money, as long as you pay it off within a certain period of time (generally, by the end of the month). To get an open credit account—like American Express—you'll need an excellent credit score and to be pulling in a high amount of income.

Here are some examples of the different types of credit:

1. Line of Credit – installment account; usually granted by a bank or credit union; fixed; low-interest rates; interest starts to accumulate the day the money is borrowed
    - FUN FACT: You can claim the interest you are charged on a line of credit—but NOT a credit card—on your tax return

2. Credit Card – revolving; high-interest rates; interest-free grace period to pay back within 21 days (before next billing cycle)

    - **Secured credit cards** require collateral, or some sort of deposit so that if you cannot pay, they will be reimbursed. If you have very poor credit, you may only be able to get a secured credit card, but doing so can definitely help improve your score if you pay on time.

3. Car Loan – usually an open loan with a fixed payment until the loan date expires

4. Mortgage – installment loan; long-term commitment generally between 25 and 30 years; low-interest rates for those with good credit

Credit Scores

Now that you understand how credit works, the next step is taking control of your credit score. Credit scores are recorded by the three major **credit bureaus**—Equifax, Experian, and Transunion—organizations that lenders can consult to check a borrower's credit (otherwise, every lender would have to weigh all of each applicant's credit history information personally). Equifax is the report card that generally matters most in Canada. Each company provides a different score, calculated on a slightly different formula. Your **FICO Score** varies from bureau to bureau and offers various industry-specific scores as well (you may notice that you have a general FICO score and then separate scores for buying a car or a home). Scores range from 300 to 800+, and a score of 670 or higher is considered a good score. Your **VantageScore** uses a single model valid for all three bureaus, and more recent scoring models use the same 300 to 800+ scale. For Vantage, however, a score of 700 or above is considered good credit. FICO and Vantage put different weights on different things, but the same methods of improving your credit will work for either.

Credit scores are calculated by considering various factors; depending on the scoring model used, the weight that each factor carries may vary. Here is a general breakdown of the factors credit scoring models consider, keeping in mind that there are many different credit scoring methods.

1. Payment History (35%)
2. Credit Utilization (30%)
3. Age of Credit (15%)
4. Credit Mix (10%)
5. New Credit (10%)

Payment History

When a lender or creditor looks at your credit report, a key question they are trying to answer is, "If I extend credit to this person, will they pay it back on time?" One of the things they will take into consideration is your payment history – how you've repaid your credit in the past. Your payment history may include credit cards, retail department store accounts, installment loans, auto loans, student loans, finance company accounts, home equity loans, and mortgage loans.

Payment history will also show a lender or creditor the details on late or missed payments. Credit scoring models generally look at how late your payments were, how much was owed, and how recently and how often you missed a payment. Your credit history will also detail how many of your credit accounts have been delinquent. So, if you have 10 credit accounts, and you've had a late payment on 5 of those accounts, that ratio may negatively impact your credit score(s).

Your payment history also includes details on bankruptcies, foreclosures, wage attachments, and any accounts that have been reported to collection agencies.

NOTE: Late payments stay on your credit report for 7 years. Late payments more than 30 days beyond the due date may lead to drastic credit score decreases.

Tips:

- Always pay on time, even if it's just the minimum payment
- Avoid any type of missed payment on utilities, phone bills, or

car payments

- Check your credit score every so often to look for any irregularities.

Credit Utilization

Another factor that lenders and creditors are looking at is how much of your available credit–the "credit limit"–you are using. Lenders and creditors like to see that you can use credit responsibly and pay it off regularly. If you have a mix of credit accounts that are "maxed out," or at their limit, that may impact your credit score(s) as well.

Utilization is only based on revolving accounts like credit cards, so this is where credit card debt has the most impact on your score. The credit bureaus recommend that you use no more than 30% of your available credit. For example, if you have a credit limit of $1,000, you should only use $300 of it. This is why it's so important to have an emergency fund! If you have to use credit to pay for something major, you can easily exceed the 30% threshold and end up maxing out your card. The longer the balance stays high, the worse the impact on your credit score.

Age of Credit

This section of your credit history details how long different credit accounts have been active. Credit score calculations may consider how long both your oldest and most recent accounts have been open. Generally speaking, creditors like to see that you have a long history of responsibly paying off your credit accounts.

Credit Mix

This section is all about the diversity of your credit. Credit score calculations consider the different types of credit accounts you have, including revolving debt (such as credit cards) and installment loans (such as mortgages, home equity loans, auto loans, student loans, and personal loans). They also look at how those accounts are distributed (i.e. is it all revolving or a mix of revolving and installments?).

Another important factor is how many of each account type you have. Lenders and creditors like to see that you're able to manage multiple accounts of different types and credit scoring models may reflect this.

Putting different bills in your name and paying them on time is an easy way to see a bump in your score.

New Credit

Credit score calculations may also consider how many new credit accounts you have opened recently. New accounts may impact the length of your credit history and your total utilization. For instance, if you have a current credit limit of $1,000 and you're using $500 of it, your utilization is at 50%. But if you add another card with a $500 credit limit ($1,500 total), now you're back down to using 30%.

Getting new credit does have its drawbacks, however. **"Hard inquiries"** are official applications for credit that appear on your credit report and stay there for 2 years. **"Soft Inquiries"** do not show up on your report, so things like checking your own credit and looking for pre-qualification offers should not make your score go down.

A quick note on the difference between being pre-qualified and pre-approved:

> Pre-qualification means that you meet the lender's basic standards for granting money. It means that they *might* grant you credit if you apply. Pre-approval means that they are offering you money. If you apply, you *will* be approved.

Your credit score will determine a lot about how you move through the world. The higher your credit, the more perks you'll get, and the more frequently you'll be given the benefit of the doubt. If you lent a friend $100 and they never paid it back, would you later lend them $1,000 and expect it to be paid back? Probably not. And if they really needed it, might you not want to hold onto something of value until they pay you back, just in case they never come up with the money? Lenders feel the same way, except unlike friends and family, they do not know you or owe you anything. The good thing is that lenders want to lend you money. They only make money if you borrow. But your credit situation will have a lot to do with how much you can get and at what price.

Another key indicator of creditworthiness—which is not part of your score but will be crucial to the lender—is one's debt-to-income ratio. In short, the debt-to-income ratio is the amount you owe compared to the amount you make. If you already have $15,000 in credit card debt and you only make $20,000 a year, lenders would be taking a big risk by lending you a large sum of money. Lenders know that things like rent, utilities, and food will always be a borrower's priority, and so they want to assure that you'll have enough money to pay them as well as your other lenders. The beauty of cash comes in here. If you have enough cash—or make a high enough salary—many people will be willing to rent you an apartment or allow you to enter into another trust-based arrangement because they see that you have a consistent means of bringing in enough income to pay.

Now we've come to the flipside of credit—debt. Remember, once you receive credit, you've also created debt. It's kind of like doing someone a favor. When someone asks you to do something important for them (let's say, borrow your car), it is customary for them to owe you (the lender) a favor. Fortunately, not all debt is bad debt. Bad debt is anything you owe money on that gives you no returns. So, credit cards are bad debt—you pay a lot of money to borrow, and while you get to use whatever you're paying for in the short-term, you ultimately pay more money for it in the long-run. A car payment is a bad debt because a car becomes less valuable the minute you drive it off the lot. In short, whether a debt is good or bad is not about immediate utility, but about whether the debt will do something positive in the long term. Good debt is what someone accumulates when they borrow money to make money. So, if you borrow money to start a profitable business, the debt is good. If you invest in real estate and rent the property at a profit, that is good debt. Try to get into as little bad debt as possible.

Credit Do's and Don't's

1. DO take advantage of pre-approvals to borrow money. Every time you request money, your score takes a hit, but if a lender offers you money, there is no penalty for taking it.

2. DON'T take on more than you can handle. If you think you'll struggle to repay, do not borrow.

3. DON'T use credit to pay bills that you do not have the money for. These bills are accruing interest, making you pay more than the services or products you received.

4. DON'T pay just the minimum payment on anything—always pay more. Credit cards already charge interest rates upwards of 22%-24% for the average borrower, and if you only pay the minimum payment each month, it will only be enough to cover the interest.

   For example, if you owe $2,000 and the minimum payment each month is $25, you could theoretically pay the debt off in 80 months, or a little under 7 years. But now we add interest—let's say 24%. For each month that you owe a balance, they charge interest. At this rate, it would take you 12 years to pay off the credit card and you would have paid $2,886.99 in interest, which is more than double the original amount borrowed.

   And lastly,

5. DON'T EVER FILE FOR BANKRUPTCY. It's one of the worst things you can do with your credit. Bankruptcies remain on your credit report for 7 years, and during that period, it will be very hard to get approved for anything. When lenders see a bankruptcy, red flags go up and they will either deny you credit outright or otherwise charge you a very high-interest rate.

Credit Repair

So, what do you do if you've already messed up your credit? Fortunately, it can be repaired.

First, you should pull your credit report. You can obtain it for free once per year or pay a monthly service to get anytime access.

Next, go through the report lender by lender and see what is still outstanding and what, if anything, has gone to collections.

Then, call each of the companies and ask to set up a payment arrangement. They will usually say yes because they want to receive as much of the original sum as possible.

If the bill has already gone to collections, this means that the original lender has sold your debt. While it certainly isn't a good thing, it isn't the worst thing either. Collections agencies buy your bad debt from companies at a fraction of the cost and then chase you down to try and recover as much as possible. This means that you have room to **negotiate**.

Once you have the collection agency on the phone, you can try to do one of two things. You can **either a) set up a payment arrangement, or b) negotiate to pay a lesser amount if you pay in one sum.** It is always best to negotiate it down and pay one lump sum if at all possible.

Once the debt is paid, you receive a letter from the company showing that you paid your collection. Some companies will **send it to the major credit bureaus** for you, but you can also get the letter and send it yourself, requesting to have your score updated. Such actions show people that you're taking control of your old bad debt and that you're responsible enough to try and build your credit back up.

A few more tactics to pay down debt and raise your score:

- Each week use your credit card to buy only the things you already have money for. At the end of each week, you pay it off. So, if you buy groceries on Monday, you pay down the balance by the following Sunday. When you do this, it's almost as if you have an interest-free loan that is affecting your score.

- **The snowball effect** – the more debt you carry, the faster it snowballs into something that seems unmanageable. If you can't pay off lump sums, start by chipping away little by little. It's like the old Jamaican saying, "small axe can cut big tree." Pay off your lowest balance cards first and when a card is paid off, you split whatever you were paying each month to your other cards. This way, without additional income, you can begin to chip away at your debt.

Chapter 4

Financial Planning "Differently":

Financial Planning is Well Worth It, Eh?

Last, but not least, we come to the practice of financial planning. As we've noted before, life becomes completely different once your money starts working for you, and the best way to continue that practice later in life is to build a strong financial plan. Good financial planning requires both short-term and long-term economic goals and looks at spending habits, debt, and other assets to determine, specifically, the best means of reaching your intended goals.

Goals are a very important facet of financial planning because many of us flit from goal to goal, changing plans frequently to suit unexpected desires. The beauty of setting goals is that you may build a plan to support them, increasing your likelihood of actually reaching them. Financial planning leads to budgeting and then allocating money to determine where it goes and when. Tracking your spending is critical because especially in the debit and credit card economies, it is easy to lose track of what you actually spend money on. Do you know how much you spend monthly on food and clothes for instance? How about subscriptions like Netflix and Hulu? Little purchases add up quickly, and if you don't track where your money goes, you may find yourself struggling to pay bills on time or to repay your debts at all.

The easiest way to budget nowadays is to use some sort of budget tracker app that links to your bank account(s) so that it can analyze your purchases by category and break down how much you spend, in each, per month. Have you ever heard the phrase "Living above [or below] your means?" A strong budgeting practice will help you discover whether you're spending less than you make (below your means), exactly as much as you make (within your means), or more than you make (above your means). Budgeting will help you visualize how much you earn, how much you spend, and how much leeway you've created in your existing plan. Net Worth is another way to calculate your means. You look at what you have (including assets, cash, stocks, etc.) and compare it to what you owe (including mortgage and car payments, student loan and credit card debt, and other liabilities). If you owe more than you have, you have a negative net worth, whereas the opposite circumstance creates positive net worth. All of us should strive to get into the green on net worth, which requires new investments, debt repayment strategies, and careful budgeting.

Budgeting

It is crucial to set smart, realistic, and measurable financial goals to succeed in your plan. This means that plans should not be rash or reactive (ex. I will NOT take a loan if I get into trouble because of poor budgeting), should be feasible, meaning that the goals are actually attainable (ex. I will NOT plan to purchase a house before I can start repayment on delinquent debt), and trackable (ex. I WILL track every expense as I try to regain control over my finances). By following these principles, goals will be more easily and regularly met, allowing you to move onto even bigger objectives.

Another key aspect of budgeting is expense reduction. Most of us buy dozens of little things each month that aren't strictly necessary, and that collectively slow down our savings goals.

To reduce your expenses, I suggest you do the following:

1. Download your bank statements (from all spending accounts) for the last three months
2. Go through these statements and highlight your needs (including food, shelter, debt payments, medical expenses, and other bills) in one color
    - After you're done, add up all the money you spent on needs for each of the last three months
        - For example, if it's May, you'll look at February, March, and April; Write the **totals by month**, the **complete sum**, and then the **monthly average**):

February - $2,000
March - $2,500
April - $2,250
TOTAL: $6,750
Average: $6,750 [total] divided by 3 months = $2,250

- The average will represent your monthly needs, accounting for variations in your monthly expenses.

- If you've labeled your needs correctly, there will be very few things that can be eliminated to save money. If you find that there are several "necessities" that you can cut, add them to the "wants" list, BUT

- There are still things you can do to lower this number. Consider:

    » Making a shopping list – when we walk through the store without a plan for what we're going to buy, it's very easy to throw things in the cart that you might not otherwise get. With a list, you'll be intentional as you're walking through the store.

    » Looking for discounts or reductions of your bills – As much as we'd all love to have unlimited data on our phone plans, many of us can do with much less. If you realize that you don't come close to your data limit every month, see about how much you can save by choosing a lower plan. The same thing applies to electricity rates (in many places), debt consolidation, and even medical expenses. Especially if you're in over your head, it never hurts to ask what discounts might be available.

        - You can also consider cutting coupons for food, buying off-brand products, and checking for weekly sales.

3. In another color, highlight your wants (things you could do without, including eating out at restaurants and fast food, subscriptions, games, entertainment, and recreational activities)

» Just as you did for your needs, add up the monthly cost of your wants for the last three months, creating a monthly total, three-month total, and average

» These numbers are the easiest to change because they represent things that you can often choose to go without. As you look at your wants, consider how you can reduce costs. Perhaps you might:

- Eliminate some of your subscription services – While variety may be the spice of life, you don't really need Netflix, Hulu, Amazon Prime, Disney+, and cable. You can probably eliminate several small expenses by evaluating what you really use.

- Get a side hustle – if you're struggling to imagine how you'll go without your monthly hair appointment/trip to the barber shop, your eyelash extensions, and your manicure, see if you can teach yourself. If you have a skill that people will pay for, charge for your services and use this money to fund your wants so that they don't drain your regular budget.

- Download discount apps and look for promo codes – There are loads of websites like Honey.com, redflagdeals.com, Rakuten.com, and Flip App that will look for promo codes that might apply to your purchases. It only takes a couple of minutes (Honey even has a Google Chrome extension that checks on any purchase page), and you may be surprised to find that you can save a decent amount on shipping fees and even products themselves.

- Wait for discounts and sales – If you can't find any discounts, you can also consider waiting for sales. Check around for the best price and if the store offers sales or clearance, you may be able to get your items at a reduced cost. But maybe you're thinking, *I can't wait that long!* In that case, you should...

- Wait at least one week before making unplanned, unnecessary purchases to avoid impulse buying – We've been trained as consumers to want the newest and most advanced things. Stores like Walmart rely on the fact that most customers come in for one thing but end up picking up several others. But sometimes those desires are fleeting, and we soon discover that we want something else instead or that we don't really need it after all. For this reason, when you discover that you want something new that wasn't planned for, wait one week from the date that you considered the purchase. If you still want it in a week, there's a greater chance that you'll make use of it.
- Cook and entertain at home – This one is a hard, but necessary step if you're trying to limit expenses. If you regularly go out for drinks or go clubbing on the weekends, reduce the number of times you go out. Instead of getting fast food or takeout, cook for yourself more nights than not.

» Together, these steps can help you drastically reduce your spending, lowering your budget and allowing you to put more towards savings, debts, and other financial goals.

Understanding Your Pay (Net vs. Gross Income)

So, the key to financial planning is understanding how much you make, how much you spend, how much you owe, and how you spread that money across your different obligations. With that in mind, it's important to understand the difference between your gross pay and your net pay. Your **gross pay** is the amount that you make before any kind of deductions. When you get a job offer (let's say they tell you that you'll be making $65,000/year), this number is your gross pay – the total amount that you earn for your work. But your gross pay isn't generally what you bring home. Anyone who has ever been employed by a business (not as a contractor or freelancer) can tell you how it felt to get their first paycheck only to discover that it was less than they expected. This is because of **deductions**, or expenses that come out of your gross pay before you get any actual money. The amount you actually receive for your work is called your **net pay**.

Taxes

Maybe you're wondering, why don't I get the full amount that I earn? That hardly seems fair. While it's a natural impulse to feel that way, we have to remember that deductions can help us save costs on retirement savings and other company benefits, and also help to keep society running through taxes. Taxes were created in the first place to fund war weapons in the early 20th-century. Back in those days, taxes were temporary. Over time, however, governments realized that if people were willing to pay them in times of war, maybe they would be willing to continue paying them in times of peace. **Taxes** are the fees that we pay into society to keep public services running. If you've ever seen construction in the city of Toronto, a small portion of what you earn went to pay those workers' salaries. By taking a portion of your check each month and sending it to the government, each of us contributes to the public services that we rely on—including the post office, public schools, and government salaries, amongst other things. While not all Canadians use every single public service, taxes are the way that we collectively assure that there is enough money for all of these public goods.

There are various types of taxes including income tax, sales tax, capital gains taxes, estate taxes, and property taxes, just to name a few of the most common types. **Sales tax** is a consumption tax, the fee that customers must pay on the money they spend. All provinces charge taxes, either on a provincial (PST), federal (GST), or combined basis—called Harmonized (HST). **Capital gains tax** applies to investments (like those discussed in Chapter 3) and are charged when you make money on an investment through a sale (selling a stock, cashing in a bond, etc.) or via dividends (when the company pays you a portion of their quarterly earnings). **Estate taxes** apply to inheritances (when someone leaves you money or property) and must be paid by the heir (the person receiving the assets). **Property taxes** are taxes on homes, land, and other types of real estate. You have to pay them as long as you occupy the property unless you become exempt from disability, age, or military status.

All of the above taxes apply to the money you spend and the things that you acquire. **Income tax**, specifically, is the tax you pay on the money you make and the things that you earn. Income tax is charged at two different levels: **provincial tax** and **federal tax**. Provincial taxes are set by each province, but for that reason, tax rates vary by location, leading to an uneven distribution of public resources. Federal tax, however, is determined by tax brackets. **Tax brackets** are the income ranges that determine how much tax you owe. So, state tax is based on where you live, while federal tax is based on what you make.

Taxes are important to understand because they help you see where your money is going and help you to understand why you don't get to keep everything you earn. This brings us back to deductions and net pay.

There are 3 basic deductions that will be taken out of your gross pay before you receive the net sum: Income tax (federal and provincial), CPP—Canadian Pension plan, and EI—Employment insurance. CPP is a taxable monthly benefit that replaces part of your income when you retire. Employment Insurance (EI) offers temporary income support to unemployed workers while they look for employment or upgrade their skills.

So, let's say that your gross income is $1,000 per month ($12,000/year) and you pay income tax at 9.5%, CPP tax at 5.25%, and EI tax at 1.58%

The calculations for your net pay would look something like this:

$1,000 earnings x 9.5% tax = (1000/.095) = $95 in taxes per month ($1,140/year)

$1,000 earnings x 5.25% tax = (1000/.0525) = $52.50 in taxes per month ($630/year)

$1,000 earnings x 1.58% tax = (1000/.0158) = $15.80 in taxes per month ($189.60/year)

This adds up to $163.30 in monthly deductions, for a total net pay of $836.70. This translates to $10,040.40 per year.

Taxes support the public good, but fortunately or unfortunately, they aren't something that you can opt-out of. Taxes are mandated by law, and therefore if you don't pay your taxes, the government will freeze your money (and sometimes even attach your salary—or take some of your paycheck as a deduction before you get it) and continue to add interest, making it more difficult to pay off. Remember, if you live at or above your means, costly tax bills can really set you back if not handled right away.

Taxes also have another personal benefit – business expenses can be written off (or counted towards the amount you earned), decreasing what you owe overall. The wealthy already know this, and therefore have found ways to claim much of their incomes/expenses as business-related. If you're self-employed, you can also make great use of this because you can justify many things as necessary for your business. For instance, if you require a car to conduct business, you can write it off on your taxes at the end of the year. This means that the gas, the car insurance, and the car payment are deducted from what you spent and what you owe. Using the tax system to your benefit reduces financial disruptions to your life.

Retirement Savings

Retirement savings are critical as well. Since people are living longer these days, we all need to plan for the future. Especially because getting older costs money and reduces our capacity to work, we want to make sure that we have it before we need it. That is what an RRSP is for. A Registered Retirement Savings Plan, or Retirement Savings Plan, is a type of tax-deferred financial account for holding savings and investment assets. The money you contribute from your gross pay will not be taxed until you withdraw it (and at a lower rate), and while there are severe penalties for withdrawing the principal early, they may also be used towards the down payment on a home.

There are really only two ways to get rich: OPM (other people's money) and OPT (other peoples' time). OPT is the principle behind business—that I can pay people to do a job at a cheaper enough rate that my time is more valuable (otherwise, you'd likely do it yourself). OPM comes in the form of investments and lines of credit. For investments, we put our money in a savings account, or stocks, or mutual funds, and those companies oftentimes lend it to other people. That's how they make money. We can also take advantage of OPM by investing with a line of credit. Whereas your credit card APR might be 22%-24%, a bank loan (for someone with good credit) may charge between 6%-8%. You can both pay off your loan at a lower rate and claim the interest on your line of credit on your taxes. With such refinancing solutions, you can increase your assets quite a bit.

Checks Over Strikes would like to thank you all for purchasing the 1st installment of the "Don't Be A Waste Yute," Financial Literacy guide. Your support and willingness to change the narrative is appreciated and vital. Our hope is that you are able to apply these fundamental principals to your everyday life. Read this book and then read it again! Make notes and put your plan on paper. This book can kickstart your journey to financial freedom. Don't delay—break the cycle today!

APPENDIX A—Glossary

Asset Classes – Types of investments

Bankruptcy – A financial status where debts are forgiven but credit is unavailable for a period of seven years

Bonds – Individual loan to companies and governments that pay interest and return the principal at a fixed interval

Capital Gains – Profits from the sale of an asset (like stocks, bonds, or real estate)

Certificate of Deposit (CDs) – A "loan" made to your bank or credit union that will be repaid over a fixed period of time and pay a fixed interest rate return

Credit – An agreement where someone (the borrower) receives something of value and agrees to repay the other party (the lender) at or by an agreed-upon date in the future

- **APR (Annual Percentage Rate)** – the annual cost of borrowing money from a certain lender; interest rate
- **Credit Bureaus** – Organizations that calculate credit scores and make them available to lenders (Transunion, Equifax, and Experian)
- **Compound Interest** – Addition of interest to the principal sum; Interest paid on interest
- **Fixed Interest** – An interest rate that does not change over time
- **Installment Accounts** – Credit accounts that have a set due date for repayment (i.e. mortgages, bank loans, car payments, etc.)
- **Interest** – a fee for borrowing charged to the borrower as an incentive to the lender
- **Open Credit** – an account where you can spend an unlimited amount but must pay it back within a set number of days—usually 30 (i.e. American Express)

- **Revolving Credit** – Credit accounts that can be used over and over once the balance has been paid down (i.e. credit cards)
- **Secured Credit Cards** – Credit cards that require collateral; usually for people with poor credit or no credit and can, therefore, help rebuild your credit.
- **Soft & Hard Inquiries** – Inquiries represent the times you have requested credit. Soft inquiries are not reflected in your score (e.g. pre-qualification); Hard inquiries are reflected in your score
- **Variable Interest** – An interest rate that changes with the market

Creditworthiness – The determination of whether or not you deserve/can be trusted with credit

Credit Report – A complete record of your credit transactions including requests, balances, delinquencies, defaults, and collections, as well as the amount of debt and payment history

Credit Score – A numerical record (like a report card) that helps lenders determine your creditworthiness

- **FICO Score** – a single-bureau score that varies from bureau to bureau
- **Vantage Score** – a tri-bureau credit score that can be used by all three bureaus

Collateral – Money or assets offered in exchange for credit used to cover losses in case of default

Credit Repair – The process of attempting to raise your credit score by paying off debts and disputing items on your credit report

Day Trading – A high-risk practice of buying and selling the same stocks on a daily basis to earn quick gains

Debt – Debt is the obligation created by borrowing money; a sum owed

Deductions – Sums that come out of your paycheck before taxes;

also, reductions you can claim on your income taxes

Default – A credit status indicating that payment has not been made on time

Diversification – Investing in several types of assets to mitigate risk

Dividends – Company profits distributed quarterly to shareholders

Emergency Fund – A savings account with three to six month's income saved for emergency expenses ONLY

Equity – Collateral value of an asset

Gross Pay – Full amount paid before any deductions

Mutual Funds – Collections of assets into which individuals can buy

Net Pay – The amount you take home from your pay after deductions

Needs v. Wants – Your necessities (food, clothing, shelter) versus your desires (shopping, entertainment, etc.)

Principal – Initial investment

Real Estate – Property including land and buildings

Registered Education Savings Plan (RESP) – An investment vehicle available to caregivers to save for their children's post-secondary education. The principal advantages of RESP's are the access they provide to the Canada Education Savings Grant and their ability to generate tax-deferred income.

Return on Investment (ROI) – Net profit on an initial investment

Risk Tolerance – A measure of how much a person can afford to lose on an investment

Registered Retirement Savings Plan (RRSP) – A type of financial account for holding savings and investment assets

Securities – Tradable financial assets

Speculation – People's public opinions about what the company will be worth

Stocks – Publicly available portions of a company for sale on the stock market

- **Stock Market** – Marketplace for buying and selling shares
- **Stockbroker** – Someone who is paid to buy and sell stocks for their clients
- **Share** – Individual piece of a company for sale; price & dividends are usually per share

Taxes – Fees assessed on purchases and income, many of which go to funding public projects, government salaries, and city maintenance

- **Capital Gains Tax** – Tax paid on money gained from profits on sold assets and dividends
- **Estate Tax** – Tax paid on inheritance by the heir
- **Exemptions** – Businesses, people, and organizations that do not have to pay taxes because of status (e.g. disability, military status, non-profit status, etc.)
- **Federal Tax** – Determined by the federal government and pays for federal programs; Assessed by tax brackets
- **Income Tax** – Tax paid on earned income
- **Property Tax** – Tax paid on the purchase and ownership of land and property
- **Provincial Tax** – Determined by the provinces and pays for provincial programs; Assessed by location
- **Sales Tax** – Tax paid on purchases
- **Tax Brackets** – Ranges of income that are assigned separate tax rates to try and collect more from those who have more and vice versa

APPENDIX B— List of Side Hustles

1. Food or Grocery Delivery Service (Instacart, Uber Eats, Skip the Dishes)
2. Virtual Assistant Service
3. Teaching English Online
4. Customer Interviews
5. Online Surveys
6. Flipping Items for Profit on Kijiji or letgo
7. Driving (Uber or Lyft)
8. Airbnb Hosting or Co-Hosting
9. Renting Out Your Car
10. Selling on Amazon
11. Private Labeling
12. Online Instruction
13. Baking
14. Bookkeeping / Accounting / Tax Preparation Service
15. Proofreading
16. E-commerce
17. Tutoring
18. Selling on Fiverr
19. Ghostwriting
20. Sports Coaching
21. Podcasting
22. Child Care
23. Caregiving
24. Building Niche Websites
25. Car Wash and Detailing
26. Catering and Cooking
27. Residential or Commercial Cleaning Service
28. Computer Repair Service
29. Consulting / Coaching
30. Cover Letter and Resume Services

APPENDIX C

52 Week Challenge - Save $1000

Week 1	Completed	Week 2	Completed	Week 3	Completed	Week 4	Completed	Week 5	Completed	Week 6
$4		$10		$53		$15		$7		$10
Week 7		Week 8		Week 9		Week 10		Week 11		Week 12
$40		$35		$31		$22		$12		$5
Week 13		Week 14		Week 15		Week 16		Week 17		Week 18
$12		$56		$5		$12		$22		$28
Week 19		Week 20		Week 21		Week 22		Week 23		Week 24
$20		$6		$28		$18		$16		$4
Week 25		Week 26		Week 27		Week 28		Week 29		Week 30
$24		$16		$24		$19		$30		$11
Week 31		Week 32		Week 33		Week 34		Week 35		Week 36
$18		$13		$37		$16		$46		$19
Week 37		Week 38		Week 39		Week 40		Week 41		Week 42
$26		$32		$10		$8		$1		$20
Week 43		Week 44		Week 45		Week 46		Week 47		Week 48
$23		$3		$13		$9		$3		$10
Week 49		Week 50		Week 51		Week 52				
$40		$30		$19		$9				

References:

Armstrong, T. (2018). Compound Interest Calculator. *Nerd Wallet*, https://www.nerdwallet.com/banking/calculator/compound-interest-calculator

Cothern, L. (2020). Investing Vs. Saving: Which Should You Do, When, And How? Money Under 30, https://www.moneyunder30.com/investing-vs-saving

"CPP retirement pension: Overview," *The Government of Canada,* https://www.canada.ca/en/services/benefits/publicpensions/cpp.html

"Employment Insurance (EI)," *The Government of Canada*, https://www.canada.ca/en/employment-social-development/programs/ei.html

Shen, L. (2017). If You Invested in Amazon at Its IPO, You Would Be a Millionaire Today. *Fortune*, https://fortune.com/2017/05/15/amazon-stock-20-years-ipo/

Made in the USA
Monee, IL
05 November 2026

68020973R00038